# RETHINK RECOVERY

## A HANDBOOK

**Conservative Care, Inc.**

*Rethink Recovery: A Handbook*

Conservative Care Inc.

Copyright © 2016. All Rights Reserved

No part of this document may be reproduced or transmitted in any form or by any means, electronic, mechanical, photocopying, recording or otherwise, without prior permission of Conservative Care Inc

Requests for permission to make copies of any part of the work should be submitted to the publisher at:

Michael Mackniak, JD.
750 Straits Tpke., Unit 2c,
Middlebury, CT 06762
MichaelMackniak.com

Cover/interior design: www.TheBookProducer.com

Printed in the USA.

First Printing

ISBN – 978-0-9974214-1-5

The material in this book cannot substitute for professional advice; further, the author is not liable if the reader relied on the material and was financially damaged in some manner.

FOR AUSTIN, BRANDON,
EMILY AND KELLY

# A WISH

MAY YOU NOTICE THE SOARING BIRDS

MAY YOU APPRECIATE THEIR GRACE

MAY YOU BE PRESENT

MAY YOU REWARD YOURSELF

MAY YOU SPARE ME A THOUGHT

MAY YOU BE GROUNDED

MAY YOU SOAR

# WEEK 1
# ACKNOWLEDGEMENT V. ACTION

# WEEK 2
## REVERSE APOLOGIES

# WEEK 3
# FAILING AT MYSELF

# WEEK 4

## TAKE WEIGHT FROM MY PLATE

WEEK 5

## MY DECISIONS ARE MY OWN

# WEEK 6
## IMPART OR IMPORT A VALUE OR A VISION

# WEEK 7

# I DRINK THEREFORE I AM

# WEEK 8
## SHAME V. GUILT
**GUILT INTENSITY • GUILT DURATION
GUILT CONTEXT • AVOIDING GUILT**

# WEEK 9

## AWFUL PEOPLE DO NOT FEEL BAD ABOUT DOING AWFUL THINGS

# WEEK 10
## SELF BLAME RESULTS IN A DESIRE TO FIX

# WEEK 11

## RITUALISTIC USE PATTERNS

# WEEK 12
## WHAT IS MY HAPPINESS

# WEEK 13
# SELF DEFEATING THOUGHTS

# WEEK 14
## REGULATING EMOTION

# WEEK 15
## BE PRESENT

# WEEK 16
## WHAT'S IN MY BLIND SPOT

# WEEK 17
## CBT:
### THOUGHTS · FEELINGS BEHAVIOR

# WEEK 18

## DO NOT BELIEVE EVERYTHING YOU THINK

# WEEK 19

## I SUFFERED A LOT IN MY LIFE BUT, NONE OF IT EVER REALLY HAPPENED
## – H.D. THOREAUX

# WEEK 20
## WE CONSTANTLY "SHOULD" ALL OVER OURSELVES

# WEEK 21

## WILL YOU HAVE THE WILL TO DO OR NOT TO DO? IF NOT, DO YOU HAVE A WILL?

# WEEK 22

## HAS DRUG/ALCOHOL EVER TRULY ENHANCED YOUR LIFE?

# WEEK 23
# ADDICTION IS AN ABUSIVE RELATIONSHIP

# WEEK 24
# ABSTINENCE

# WEEK 25

## I HAVE MET YOU AND SO I WILL NEVER BE THE SAME PERSON AGAIN.

# WEEK 26
## PHASES OF CHANGE
**PRECONTEMPLATION • CONTEMPLATION
PREPARATION • ACTION • MAINTENANCE**

# WEEK 27
# KNOW YOU CAN SAY NO

# WEEK 28

## WHICH CHOICE DRUG IS CHOOSING YOU?

# WEEK 29

## PLAY FORWARD YOUR OWN MOVIE

# WEEK 30

## REPLACING ADDICTION WITH ADDICTION

# WEEK 31
## INTERNAL SHAME AND SELF DOUBT

# WEEK 32

## TO BE CONSTANTLY ANGRY IS TO HARM ONE'S SOUL

# WEEK 33

## I HAVE TOO MANY NEVERS
## – SEAN KELLY

# WEEK 34

## THERE IS SOMETHING MYSTIC IN RECOVERY

# WEEK 35

## IF YOU DO NOT HAVE EXPECTATIONS YOU CANNOT HAVE DISAPPOINTMENT

# WEEK 36

## EXTREME TOLERANCE IS IGNORING ONE'S NEEDS

# WEEK 37

## WHICH WOLF ARE YOU FEEDING

# WEEK 38
## GO TO BED WITH YOURSELF

# WEEK 39

## ARE YOU AVOIDING HELL OR CLIMBING OUT OF IT?

# WEEK 40
## RELIGIOUS V. SPIRITUAL

# WEEK 41

## EGO:

**BODY • AVOID FEAR • AVOID FAILURE
AVOID PAIN • AVOID LOSS**

# WEEK 42
## SPIRIT:
### SELF • NURTURE
### LIVE • ACT

# WEEK 43

## BELIEF BRINGS CHILDREN COMFORT AND JOY

# WEEK 44

## ONLY DO IN THE DARK WHAT YOU WOULD DO IN THE LIGHT

# WEEK 45
## PLAY

# WEEK 46

## WHAT WOULD YOUR MOTHER THINK?

# WEEK 47
# NOTHING DOESN'T CHANGE

# WEEK 48

## MEASURE YOURSELF BY WHAT YOU WILL DO

# WEEK 49

## DO YOU HAVE THE RIGHT TO BE HAPPY?

# WEEK 50

## THINGS ARE NEVER AS BAD AS THE WORST

# WEEK 51

## CAN WE BE BETTER THAN THE BEST?

# WEEK 52
## PURPOSEFUL GUILT

www.ingramcontent.com/pod-product-compliance
Lightning Source LLC
Chambersburg PA
CBHW052136010526
44113CB00036B/2283